THE WARTHOGS

Fascinating Facts, Habitats, and Behaviors of Nature's Toughest Survivor

Scott M. Cook

Table of Contents

Introduction

The Warthog's Secret World

Hidden among the golden grasses of Africa's savannas, a creature often overlooked roams with a quiet confidence. Its tusks curve like nature's scythes, its mane bristles like a warrior's crest, and its sharp eyes betray a cunning intelligence. Meet the warthog—a creature that might seem like a peculiar oddity but is, in fact, one of nature's most remarkable survivors.

At first glance, a warthog may not capture the admiration granted to its more majestic neighbors like lions or elephants. However, dig a little deeper, and you'll uncover an animal packed with surprises. These resilient creatures have evolved to not only survive but thrive in some of the most unforgiving environments on Earth. Their lives are a testament to adaptability, resourcefulness, and an unyielding will to endure.

In this book, we'll explore the many facets of warthogs—from their intriguing behaviors to their unique place in the animal kingdom. What makes these animals so fascinating? Is it their ability to face down predators many times their size, their ingenious use of burrows for safety, or the unexpected tenderness they show toward their young? Perhaps it's all these things and more. As we journey through their world, you'll discover just how much there is to admire about these tough yet charming creatures.

Warthogs are more than just wild pigs with tusks—they're a vital part of the ecosystems they inhabit. Their story is one of resilience, often misunderstood but undeniably captivating. Let's step into the savanna and get to know one

of nature's toughest survivors. The rest
of their story is waiting to unfold.

Chapter 1: Overview of Warthogs

This chapter will lay the foundation for understanding warthogs by exploring their general characteristics, ecological role, and what sets them apart from other animals.

Introduction to Warthogs

Warthogs may not wear the crown of the savanna's king, but they've carved out a unique place in the wild that demands respect. As members of the pig family, they are often underestimated, dismissed as mere scavengers or comic relief in the grand tapestry of African wildlife. But these animals are far more complex than they appear.

Scientifically known as *Phacochoerus africanus*, warthogs are native to sub-Saharan Africa. Their ancestors roamed these lands for millions of years, adapting and evolving to survive in an environment fraught with challenges. Today, they are known for their rugged features, quick reflexes, and remarkable ability to outwit predators.

Key Characteristics

Physically, warthogs are striking. Their stocky bodies, covered in sparse hair, are built for both power and endurance. Their most iconic feature, the tusks, serve as both a defensive weapon and a tool for foraging. These curved ivory protrusions can grow impressively large, making them a formidable opponent to those who dare threaten them. Adding to their distinct appearance is their mane—a bristly ridge running along their spine—that gives them a wild, almost defiant look.

Why They're Fascinating

But warthogs are more than their appearance. They are essential contributors to their ecosystem. By grazing on tough grasses and using their snouts to dig for roots, they help maintain the balance of their habitat. Their abandoned burrows often provide shelter for other animals, showcasing how even their most mundane habits have a ripple effect in the wild.

Perhaps what's most fascinating about warthogs is their ability to thrive in adversity. Whether it's facing down a predator or enduring the dry season when food is scarce, warthogs embody resilience. They may not be the largest or the most glamorous creatures on the savanna, but their story is one of grit, adaptability, and survival.

Chapter 2: Warthogs in the Animal Kingdom

In this chapter, you'll gain an in-depth understanding of how warthogs fit into the broader animal kingdom. We'll start by exploring their classification and evolutionary journey, shedding light on how these fascinating animals have adapted over time to survive in the wild. You'll discover the unique features that make them stand out from other animals in their environment. From their distinctive tusks to their social behavior, this chapter will highlight the traits that have helped warthogs thrive where many others struggle.

Classification and Evolution

Warthogs are a fascinating example of the diverse family of pigs, but they are not your average pig. They belong to the *Suidae* family, which includes animals such as wild boars and domesticated pigs. Specifically, they belong to the genus *Phacochoerus*, with the species *Phacochoerus africanus* commonly known as the common warthog.

The evolutionary journey of warthogs is one of adaptability and resilience. Their ancestors first appeared millions of years ago and have since evolved to thrive in the harsh conditions of Africa's savannas and woodlands. Over time, warthogs have developed traits that enhance their ability to survive in these challenging environments. Their large tusks and muscular bodies, for example, are products of an evolutionary process designed to help them defend against predators and compete for resources.

Unique Traits Compared to Other Animals

What sets warthogs apart from other animals in the wild is their blend of physical features, social behavior, and survival strategies. One of the most remarkable traits is their tusks—these sharp, curved teeth serve multiple purposes. Not only do they help warthogs defend themselves from predators like lions and hyenas, but they are also used to dig for food.

Unlike many other animals, warthogs can often be seen running into burrows at high speed to escape danger. Their ability to dive into these underground shelters shows their incredible reflexes and awareness of their surroundings. Unlike the larger and slower animals in their habitat, warthogs have adapted to rely on speed and cunning rather than brute strength.

Another unique feature is their social behavior. Warthogs typically live in small family groups, known as sounders, led by a dominant female. These groups offer protection against predators and support in finding food. However, unlike other herd animals, warthogs are not known for forming large, cohesive groups. Their social structure is more fluid, allowing them to adapt to different environments and threats.

These remarkable adaptations have allowed warthogs to survive in some of the harshest conditions on Earth. By blending strength, agility, and keen instincts, they stand out as one of the animal kingdom's most enduring survivors.

Chapter 3: Physical Characteristics

In this chapter, we'll look into the physical attributes that make warthogs unique and perfectly suited to their environments. You'll discover why their tusks are not only for defense but also for survival in their day-to-day lives. We'll also explore their distinctive mane, body shape, and other physical traits that allow them to thrive in the wild. Along the way, you'll learn how their bodies are finely tuned to help them dig for food, evade predators, and stay comfortable in some of the harshest environments on Earth. By the end of this chapter, you'll have a deeper appreciation for just how incredible

the warthog's physical features really are.

Distinctive Features (Tusks, Mane, etc.)

Warthogs are easily recognized by their most striking features: their tusks and manes. These features not only give them a distinctive appearance but are essential for their survival. The tusks, which are actually elongated canine teeth, serve multiple purposes. Male warthogs possess larger tusks than females, which they use to defend their territory, fight off predators, and compete for mates. These tusks are sharpened against the ground as warthogs dig for food or when they engage in combat with one another.

The mane, which runs along the back of a warthog's neck and extends down its spine, is another unique physical feature. This bristly, erect mane helps to make the warthog appear larger when it is threatened. The mane also plays a role in the animal's cooling system, helping to regulate body temperature by providing some protection from the sun.

Warthogs also have tough, wrinkled skin that is not only a visual characteristic but a protective one. The folds of skin around their faces and necks shield them from scratches and bites. Their large, flat feet are also well-suited for traversing rough terrain, allowing them to move swiftly across rocky, uneven ground and escape predators.

Adaptations for Survival

Every aspect of the warthog's body has evolved to help it survive in the wild. One of the most important adaptations is their strong, muscular frame.

Warthogs can run at speeds of up to 30 miles per hour, which is faster than most of their predators. This speed, coupled with their ability to quickly dart into burrows, gives them an advantage when escaping danger.

Warthogs also have sharp senses of hearing and smell, which help them detect approaching predators long before they are seen. Their ability to dig quickly for roots, tubers, and grasses is aided by their powerful forelimbs and specialized, shovel-like hooves, allowing them to find food in even the most arid environments.

Their ability to live in a wide range of habitats—everything from savannas to open woodlands—can be attributed to their adaptable diet and physical traits. Whether it's running across a hot savanna or sheltering in a burrow during a storm, the warthog's body is built to thrive in the toughest environments.

Chapter 4: Habitats and Range

In this chapter, you'll explore the natural habitats of warthogs and where they can be found around the world. We'll take a closer look at the regions they call home, from the savannas of Africa to the woodland areas and other less-known ecosystems. You'll learn about the types of environments warthogs prefer and how their behaviors and physical features allow them to thrive in these diverse habitats. By the end of this chapter, you'll gain a better understanding of the geographic range of warthogs and how they've adapted to various climates and terrains.

Where Warthogs Live

Warthogs are native to sub-Saharan Africa, with their range extending across much of the continent. These resilient animals are found in a variety of countries, including South Africa, Namibia, Kenya, Tanzania, and Uganda, to name just a few. They primarily inhabit savannas, grasslands, and open woodlands, where the environment provides a mixture of both cover and food.

Though they prefer wide, open areas, warthogs are also known to inhabit regions with varying amounts of vegetation, as long as there is ample space for them to dig and forage for food. They can even be found in more arid, semi-desert areas, as long as there is access to water and enough plant life to sustain their diet. Warthogs are often seen in game reserves and national parks, where their populations are protected, allowing them to roam freely in their natural environment.

Environmental Preferences

Warthogs tend to favor flat, open areas where they can easily spot predators from a distance, but they also need some cover to shelter from the harsh sun or seek refuge when necessary. They tend to stay close to watering holes, which provide both hydration and a place to cool down. The availability of food is also a critical factor in their choice of habitat. They thrive in places where grasses, roots, and tubers are abundant, as well as areas with access to seasonal rainfall that helps support the plant life they rely on.

Though they are adaptable to different environments, warthogs prefer areas with relatively mild temperatures. Extreme heat or intense cold can be challenging for them. In areas where the climate is harsh, warthogs have developed the ability to burrow into the earth to escape both predators and extreme weather conditions. Their dens, often created in abandoned burrows of other animals, offer them a safe haven from the elements and predators.

Warthogs also show some level of migration in response to the availability of resources. During the dry season, they may travel further in search of food and water, often following the movements of other herbivores. This adaptability in their habitat selection is key to their survival, as it allows them to thrive in a variety of landscapes.

Chapter 5: Behaviors and Social Life

This chapter delves into the fascinating behaviors of warthogs and how they interact with one another. You'll learn about their unique feeding habits, including their resourceful methods of foraging and their ability to adapt to different diets based on environmental conditions. We'll also explore the social lives of warthogs, uncovering how they communicate, form bonds, and structure their groups. By the end of this chapter, you'll have a deeper understanding of what makes warthogs such intriguing animals in the wild.

Feeding Habits

Warthogs are primarily grazers, with a diet consisting of grasses, roots, tubers, and fruits. They are known for their remarkable ability to dig into the ground using their snouts and tusks to unearth food sources such as roots and bulbs, which provide essential nutrients. This foraging behavior not only helps them sustain themselves during dry seasons when surface vegetation is scarce but also plays a role in soil aeration, benefiting the ecosystems they inhabit.

Warthogs are not picky eaters. While they prefer fresh grasses and tender shoots, they have been observed eating bark, small animals, and even carrion when food is scarce. Their ability to adapt their diet to what is available is a testament to their resilience as survivors. Warthogs often graze on their knees, a distinctive behavior that helps them reach shorter grasses and reduces the strain on their bodies during prolonged feeding sessions.

Social Structures and Communication

Warthogs are highly social animals, living in groups called sounders. A typical sounder is composed of a few females and their offspring, while adult males tend to lead more solitary lives, joining groups temporarily during mating seasons. These groups provide safety in numbers, with members watching out for predators and sounding alarms when danger is near.

Communication within a sounder is achieved through a variety of vocalizations, body language, and even scent marking. Warthogs are known to emit grunts, squeals, and snorts to convey emotions such as distress, contentment, or aggression. They also rely on their tails, which are often held upright like flags, to signal to one another when moving as a group.

The hierarchy within a sounder is usually led by the dominant female, who guides the group to feeding and resting spots. Despite their tough exterior, warthogs display nurturing behavior, with mothers fiercely protecting their young from predators and teaching them survival skills. Young warthogs engage in playful activities, which not only strengthen their bonds but also prepare them for adult life in the wild.

Warthogs have a fascinating way of showing respect and submission within their groups. For instance, subordinate warthogs will lower their heads or lie down in the presence of a dominant individual. This structured interaction helps maintain harmony within the group, ensuring the survival of all members.

Chapter 6: Challenges in the Wild

This chapter uncovers the challenges warthogs face in their natural environments. From evading apex predators to navigating the threats posed by human encroachment, warthogs have developed remarkable survival strategies. We'll explore how they defend themselves and the critical role of conservation efforts in mitigating human-wildlife conflicts. By the end, you'll appreciate the resilience of warthogs and the delicate balance needed to ensure their survival in the wild.

Predators

In the African savanna, warthogs face a host of natural predators, including lions, leopards, cheetahs, hyenas, and crocodiles. These formidable hunters often target warthogs due to their moderate size and abundance. However, warthogs are not defenseless; they possess an impressive arsenal of survival tactics.

When confronted by predators, warthogs rely on their speed and agility to escape. They can run at speeds of up to 30 miles per hour, zigzagging to confuse their pursuers. Their sharp tusks are also potent weapons, capable of inflicting serious injuries on attackers. A cornered warthog can become surprisingly aggressive, charging at predators with its tusks to defend itself and its young.

Burrows serve as critical refuges for warthogs. They often occupy abandoned aardvark burrows, modifying them to suit their needs. When threatened, warthogs will reverse into these burrows, leaving their sharp tusks facing outward to deter predators. This behavior has proven highly effective against many would-be attackers.

Despite their vigilance, young warthogs (piglets) are especially vulnerable to predators. Mothers display extraordinary bravery, risking their lives to protect their offspring. Their maternal instincts include charging at predators or distracting them to ensure the piglets have a chance to escape.

Human-Wildlife Conflict

As human populations expand, warthogs increasingly find themselves at odds with agricultural activities. Farmers often view them as pests due to their tendency to raid crops, which can lead to significant economic losses.

In retaliation, warthogs are sometimes hunted or trapped, further straining their populations.

Habitat destruction poses another significant threat. The clearing of land for agriculture, urban development, and infrastructure reduces the availability of food and shelter for warthogs. This forces them to venture closer to human settlements, exacerbating conflicts.

Poaching, though not as prevalent for warthogs as for other species, still occurs. Warthogs are hunted for their meat, which is considered a delicacy in some regions, and for their tusks, which are used as trophies or ornaments.

Fortunately, conservation efforts are underway to address these challenges. Wildlife reserves and national parks provide safe havens where warthogs can thrive without interference. Educational campaigns aim to foster coexistence by teaching communities about the ecological benefits of warthogs, such as their role in maintaining soil health and controlling vegetation.

Collaborative projects between conservationists and local communities are also helping to mitigate conflicts. For example, some programs promote the use of non-lethal deterrents, such as fencing or natural repellents, to protect crops without harming warthogs.

Chapter 7: Fun and Lesser-Known Facts

This chapter takes a lighter, fascinating look at warthogs, showcasing their role in folklore, myths, and cultural significance across different societies. You'll also uncover some of their most remarkable survival skills and quirky behaviors, providing a deeper appreciation for these resilient animals. Prepare to learn things about warthogs that you never imagined!

Myths and Cultural Significance

Across Africa and beyond, warthogs feature prominently in myths and traditions, often embodying unique symbolic meanings. In some cultures, warthogs are revered as symbols of strength and tenacity due to their fearless nature and ability to thrive in harsh environments.

Folklore across various regions often portrays warthogs as cunning and resourceful creatures. One tale from East Africa tells of a warthog outsmarting a lion by luring it into a narrow burrow and trapping it inside. This story emphasizes the warthog's intelligence and quick thinking, traits that many communities respect and admire.

In other areas, warthogs are seen as guardians of the wild. Their habit of maintaining and enlarging burrows has led some to believe they play a spiritual role in protecting the land. Local legends often attribute their burrow-digging behaviors to divine guidance, viewing them as nature's engineers.

However, not all perceptions are positive. In some myths, warthogs are depicted as mischievous or unlucky animals. This duality reflects the complex relationship humans have had with warthogs throughout history.

Amazing Survival Skills

Warthogs possess some of the most remarkable survival skills in the animal kingdom. Their ability to adapt to various challenges has earned them the title of nature's toughest survivors. Here are a few surprising facts about these incredible animals:

- **A Built-in Alarm System**
  Warthogs have an exceptional sense of hearing and smell, which they use to detect predators from great distances. Their acute senses often alert other animals

in the area, making them valuable members of the savanna ecosystem.

- **Kneeling to Eat**
One of the most unusual behaviors of warthogs is their habit of kneeling while grazing. This peculiar posture helps them access low-lying grasses and roots, ensuring they can feed efficiently even in sparse environments. Their calloused forelegs are specially adapted for this purpose.

- **Masters of Burrow Borrowing**
Instead of digging their own burrows, warthogs are experts at repurposing abandoned ones, particularly those left behind by aardvarks. This ingenious

strategy saves energy and
provides instant shelter,
showcasing their opportunistic
nature.

- **Water-Wise Warriors**
  During dry seasons, warthogs
  exhibit incredible resourcefulness
  by surviving on minimal water.
  Their bodies are adapted to
  conserve moisture, enabling them
  to endure arid conditions that
  would challenge many other
  animals.

- **Social Savvy**
  Despite their rugged appearance,
  warthogs are highly social
  animals. They communicate
  through a range of grunts,
  squeals, and tail movements,
  displaying a level of social

intelligence that often goes unnoticed.

- **Remarkable Memory**
Warthogs have been observed remembering safe burrow locations and areas with abundant food for years, demonstrating their impressive memory skills. This ability significantly boosts their survival in fluctuating environments.

Conclusion

The warthog, often overlooked and underestimated, is a remarkable animal that exemplifies resilience, intelligence, and adaptability. From their distinctive physical features and unique survival strategies to their complex social lives and cultural significance, warthogs offer an endless source of fascination. They are much more than their rugged appearance; they are nature's unsung heroes, thriving in environments where many others would falter.

Through this book, we've explored their journey in the animal kingdom, delving into their habitats, behaviors, and challenges in the wild. We've uncovered the myths and facts that make warthogs a cultural and ecological treasure, highlighting their vital role in their ecosystems and their ability to adapt and survive against the odds.

As you've read through these chapters, we hope you've gained a newfound appreciation for these tough and tenacious creatures. Whether you're an animal enthusiast, a conservation advocate, or simply curious about the natural world, the warthog's story reminds us of the incredible diversity and ingenuity of life on Earth.

Let this book serve as both a tribute to the warthog and an inspiration to continue learning about and protecting the amazing creatures that share our planet. The more we understand and respect the natural world, the better equipped we are to ensure its survival for generations to come.